THE DEEP DIVE

7 Life Rafts To Survive Career Currents

MATTHEW C. MEADE

Copyright © 2025 Matthew C. Meade

ISBN: 978-1-7349486-2-2 Paperback
ISBN: 978-1-7349486-3-9 Ebook

All rights reserved. No part of this book may be reproduced, stored, or transmitted by any means—whether auditory, graphic, mechanical, or electronic—without written permission of both publisher and author, except in the case of brief excerpts used in critical articles and reviews. Unauthorized reproduction of any part of this work is illegal and punishable by law.

DEDICATION

To My Family,

I express my deepest gratitude for the incredible network of support that has propelled me to this point. It is not solely through my efforts but through the combined strength of God, my mother, family, ancestors, students, colleagues, professors, teachers, sponsors, mentors, and friends. Thank you for deeming me deserving of your support and love, I appreciate it sincerely. Each one of you serves as a conduit for God's enduring presence in my journey. I aspire to make you immensely proud. I also aim to perpetuate our shared legacy with unwavering commitment.

Matthew C. Meade

COMPASS

ONE
Navigate the Deep Blue Sea *1*

TWO
Know Your Worth. *10*

THREE
Lead Through Ambiguity. *19*

FOUR
Check Your Blind Spots *30*

FIVE
Don't Procrastinate to Pivot *40*

SIX
Your Best Self Requires Self-Care *51*

SEVEN
The Rest Ashore. *61*

THE DEEP DIVE: 7 LIFE RAFTS TO SURVIVE CAREER CURRENTS

A few years ago, I embarked on a trip to Cabo San Lucas, Mexico. One of the highlights was a boat ride to witness the famous arches. The waters were a mesmerizing shade of ice blue, a gentle, warm breeze filled the air, and the sun blazed down like a scorching New York City summer day.

Periodically, the boat's captain would pause our journey, allowing passengers to capture the perfect snapshot of the breathtaking view. During these moments of stillness, we truly grasped how the wind above the water and the whales beneath us influenced the boat's swaying motion.

In many ways, this boat trip serves as a metaphor for your career journey as a professional. The azure waters, the comforting warmth of the sun, and the gentle breeze provide a fitting backdrop for the adventures and challenges ahead. There's a striking resemblance between this serene boat ride and the nuances of your career. Just as the wind, waves, and underwater wildlife made our boat sway, these elements can be likened to the unpredictable internal and external disruptions that can impact your professional path.

Much like ocean currents, which are driven by the forces of gravity, wind, and water density, careers are shaped by a multitude of factors, many of which are beyond our control. Internal factors such as your team dynamics, management style, the role not being the right fit for your skillset, or company culture can steer your career journey. Additionally, external factors like industry trends, economic shifts, or political changes can impact your experiences as well.

Sailboats, unlike the steady cruise we embarked on, can utilize these currents to their advantage when the sail is positioned a certain way. However, this doesn't mean the journey will always be smooth. The boat can be jolted and tossed around, but after the storms subside, the currents can guide you in the right direction.

It takes skill, focus, and great confidence to stay the course and recognize your port of call during your career. This book is your compass, designed to provide you with practical advice, strategies, and tactics to help you navigate the deep waters without feeling overwhelmed and to ensure you successfully arrive.

As a leader, you embody the flexibility, creativity, and perseverance necessary to traverse the ups and downs of your professional path. This book will guide you through my personal experiences and lessons learned across various stages of my career. You will be inspired to create and pursue Specific, Measurable, Achievable, Relevant, and Time-Bound (SMART) goals that are customized to your journey through seven chapters that highlight important takeaways and note-taking sections. By applying the information and practical tips found in this book, you will be able to identify and develop your innate talents and take steps toward the fulfilling and prosperous career you deserve.

NAVIGATE THE DEEP BLUE SEA

During my seventh-grade year, I attended a pool party celebrating the end of the school year with classmates at the community pool in South Orange, New Jersey. The event generated considerable excitement throughout the week, with everyone eager to participate in the festivities. I watched my friends plunging into the eight-foot section of the pool and felt the desire to join in on the fun. The warm, sunny day motivated me. "Here goes nothing," I thought as I leaped into the deep end of the pool.

Splash!

It didn't take long for me to realize the gravity of my situation. You see, I had never taken swimming lessons, and as I plunged into the deep end, panic set in. Water rushed into my nose, and I found myself flailing my arms and legs, desperately searching for a breath of air. In this tough moment, the alert lifeguard at the pool saw my predicament and jumped in to save me. They pulled me to the poolside and advised me to "catch your breath." Grateful to be back on dry land, I mustered a sincere "thank you."

This incident prompted me to dedicate considerable time to swimming lessons. A year later, I underwent a swim test—a pivotal moment. I jumped off the diving board into fourteen feet of water and earned the coveted green dot on my pool badge. This symbolized my successful test completion and permitted me to dive off of the diving board into the deep waters for the entire summer.

Your mid-level career can often feel like that moment in the deep end of the pool.

It's easy to find yourself submerged in the relentless daily grind, juggling long working hours, addressing team culture challenges, and adapting to organizational changes. Days turn into weeks, and weeks into months. Before you know it, a full year has passed, and you're overwhelmed. Lack of boundaries can lead to a feeling of drowning, similar to my experience at the seventh-grade pool party. This is when you find yourself in the "deep blue sea."

The Deep Dive

The "deep blue sea" represents the middle to executive levels of your career. Every day, you set sail from home to the deep waters of work. In these challenging depths, you navigate project demands, cross-functional collaboration, building high-performing global teams, and adapting to organizational changes. Several factors can impact your career trajectory, including job market shifts, economic factors like inflation, and the need to upskill with technology.

As you embark on your mid-level career, remember that success is not about staying afloat but mastering the art of navigation. Perform well, but don't hesitate to ask for help. This is where career lifeguards in the form of sponsors and mentors come in. They help you identify blind spots and pull you out of the deep end when you're struggling.

The lifeguard is an ally, someone you can rely on, and someone who genuinely cares for your progress. Research members of your organization with similarities in line of work, alma mater, or personal interests. Seek individuals whose values, backgrounds, and abilities align with your desired professional path. Look for mentors with a history of helping others. Attend conferences, networking events, and workplace activities to meet potential sponsors or mentors. Talk to people, share your goals, and ask for guidance.

Many firms have professional development-focused Business Resource Groups (BRGs). Join clubs that interest you to meet others with experience. They might be open to serving as your sponsor or mentor. A mentor is someone who provides guidance, advice, and support based on their own experiences. They help you develop skills, navigate challenges, and set career goals. The relationship is typically informal and focuses on personal and professional growth. Whereas, a sponsor is a senior leader or executive who actively champions your career advancement. They leverage their influence to help you get high-visibility projects, promotions, or leadership roles. The relationship is more strategic and transactional as they put their reputation on the line for you. The key differences are that mentors talk with you, and sponsors talk about you. A mentor helps you grow, while a sponsor helps you move up in an organization. You seek out mentors, but sponsors choose you based on your performance and potential.

Invite experts whose work you admire to get tea or coffee so you can have a conversation. Attend these meetings to gain additional knowledge. Describe your objectives. Find out if mentorship is an option. If your company has a structured mentorship program, explore it, as mentors and mentees are often paired based on their interests and career objectives.

Lastly, do a good job; excellent work speaks volumes. Participate in meaningful discussions and request guidance. Express gratitude for any advice received. Show your ability and dedication. This may catch the interest of sponsors or mentors. Effective sponsors and mentors are crucial for career advancement. These connections give you strategic insights and provide direction when trying to stay afloat.

A sponsor is essential to your career; they use performance currency based on how successfully you deliver assignments for them and relationship currency from your long-term partnership. People need to know who you are because sponsors will use both forms of currency to campaign on your behalf. They often appreciate excellence.

Remember, building a mentorship or sponsorship relationship takes time. It requires mutual trust and respect to navigate the "deep blue sea." Be proactive, authentic, and open to learning from others. Good luck as you navigate the deep waters with confidence and resilience.

7 LIFE RAFTS TO NAVIGATE THE DEEP BLUE SEA CAREER CURRENTS

1. **Recognize the Importance of Learning from Setbacks**: Just as I learned from the near-drowning experience, mid-level professionals must see setbacks as opportunities for growth. Whether facing workplace challenges or personal development issues, every setback can be a chance to learn and improve.

2. **Embrace the Journey of Career Development**: Much like mastering swimming skills, advancing in your career requires dedication and continuous learning. Invest time and effort in developing the skills necessary to navigate the complexities of your profession.

3. **Navigate Challenges with Strategic Thinking**: Swimming in deep waters signifies the challenges mid-level professionals face in their careers. Rather than merely staying afloat, develop strategic thinking skills to navigate obstacles effectively.

4. **Seek Support from Career Lifeguards - Mentors and Sponsors**: Just as the lifeguard provided crucial assistance in the pool, mentors and sponsors can offer guidance and support in your career. Actively seek out individuals who can provide valuable insights and help you identify blind spots.

5. **Networking is Key**: Attend company events, conferences, and networking gatherings to connect with experienced professionals who can potentially become mentors or sponsors. Engage in meaningful conversations, express your aspirations, and seek advice.

6. **Show Initiative and Gratitude**: Demonstrate your commitment to learning and growth within your organization. Seek out opportunities to engage with mentors, ask for advice, and express gratitude for any guidance received. Showing initiative and a genuine interest in personal and professional development can attract the attention of potential mentors or sponsors.

7. **Excel in Your Work**: Performance speaks volumes. Strive for excellence in your role, engage in meaningful conversations, and actively seek opportunities for advancement. By demonstrating capability and commitment, you increase your chances of attracting the support of mentors or sponsors who appreciate dedication and hard work.

3 Personal **SMART** goals to Navigate the Deep Waters (Specific, Measurable, Achievable, Relevant, and Time-Bound)

READER TAKEAWAY 1

READER TAKEAWAY 2

READER TAKEAWAY 3

NOTES

KNOW YOUR WORTH

One day, as I was leaving the office in the financial district of New York City, the clouds were thick, signaling imminent rain. There was a man on the street selling umbrellas. I asked him, "How much are the umbrellas?"

He quickly replied, "5 dollars for now."

I said, "For now?"

He replied, "Yes, the rain is coming; once the rain starts, the price will double."

Instantly, I thought about economics and the power of supply and demand. When demand is high and supply is low, prices rise. You need to think about your career the same way. As you become more seasoned and specialized through experience, your value to corporations or your own business should increase. Know your worth in the market for yourself and your family.

As you progress as a mid-level professional, you gain experience. You also hone your expertise. You become more influential to corporations or your own business. Recognizing your market value is crucial for personal growth and your family's well-being. Your career journey may involve highs and lows. During the lows, always acknowledge the worth you add, even in the deepest currents.

From the moment you start a new opportunity, it's crucial to know your identity and what you bring to the team. As you develop and reshape your identity, refine that definition. Consistently build and refine your brand by showcasing your strengths and the value you provide to the organization. To achieve optimal self-actualization in your career, reflect on what sets you apart. Your brand flourishes when others see the distinctiveness and expertise you bring to the business. This connects to your platform, showing your impact on the organization and channeling influence across the firm and access to senior-level stakeholders.

Improving the organization can speed up tasks and boost your reputation. Emulate the user-friendly approach of beloved brands by promoting seamless collaboration, partnerships, and a commitment to excellence. As you navigate in your career, keep in mind that the goal is not to master everything. Instead, focus on aligning your strengths with your passions. Address areas for improvement by hiring where needed, and crafting a career that no longer feels like work.

You must bet on yourself, your success as a coach, and your ability to empower teams and appreciate others. The journey may have challenges and setbacks, but it's important to see each one as a win or a chance to learn. Keep your "why" or North Star close at all times—it's the force behind your passion. Let it shine in all you do.

To understand your value, it is important to express it succinctly to others in your organization. Prepare a thirty-second and a sixty-second elevator pitch tailored for various situations. Your pitch should introduce your name and job, highlighting one to three key points that showcase your impact and create a connection. The outcome of a new connection can be unpredictable, potentially leading to relationships, opportunities, partnerships, or interviews. Follow up with a thoughtful "nice to meet you" email, outlining potential mutual benefits. Using this strategy has made my brand stand out and built lasting relationships with bank executives.

To fully display your value in organizations, you need to understand the firm. Learn the company's mission, vision, and goals to ensure your work aligns with them. Additionally, showcasing your achievements involves quantifying your impact. Use specific metrics to highlight the tangible results of your efforts, such as meeting deadlines, successful projects, increased client adoption, or higher revenue. Keep a detailed record of your accomplishments, successful projects, and positive feedback. Use this documentation during reviews or career advancement discussions. It provides a log of your monthly contributions.

Seek feedback from colleagues, supervisors, and team members. Constructive input can show where to improve. It also underscores your dedication to growth and development. Volunteering for projects and assignments that fit your skills and interests shows initiative and a willingness to go above and beyond, both of which help the organization succeed.

Finally, focus on professional development. Stay updated on industry trends. Attend relevant workshops or training programs. Get certifications that enhance your expertise. Demonstrating a commitment to growth enhances your professional profile.

When showing your value, it's crucial to grasp the 3 P's: performance, presence, and platform.

Performance pertains to your skill in completing tasks within the organization. Presence reflects your ability to instill confidence in others, lead by example, and inspire others to follow you. Finally, the platform represents the path to the next level, based on your ability to manage people or handle crucial tasks. To excel, you must embody all 3 P's. Having only two out of three may make you an average professional. Having one out of three could limit you. Use these three factors to assess if you are ready to lead through ambiguity and pivot when needed.

Your career journey is a series of choices and opportunities. It's vital to acknowledge your worth at every step. Embrace self-confidence, articulate your value, and recognize your unique strengths and passions. This self-awareness will empower you to navigate your work's complexities with great perseverance.

 **7 LIFE RAFTS TO NAVIGATE CAREER CURRENTS BY KNOWING YOUR WORTH**

1. **Recognize Your Value Proposition**: As you gain experience and expertise, your value to corporations or your own business should increase. Knowing your worth in the market is crucial for personal growth and ensuring your family's well-being.

2. **Define Your Identity and Brand**: Define who you are and refine your identity as you develop within organizations. Showcase your strengths and unique contributions to build and refine your brand.

3. **Make Sure to Quantify Your Impact**: Use specific metrics to quantify your impact and maintain a record of accomplishments, successful projects, and positive feedback.

4. **Craft a Compelling Elevator Pitch**: Prepare concise elevator pitches tailored for different situations to succinctly express your value and make connections. Follow up with new connections to further solidify relationships and explore potential opportunities.

5. **Embody the 3 P's: Performance, Presence, and Platform:** Excel in completing tasks (performance), instill confidence in others (presence), and demonstrate readiness for the next level (platform). Strive to embody all 3 P's to excel in your career and navigate challenges with resilience.

6. **Bet on Yourself and Success**: Have confidence in your abilities as a coach and empower others. View challenges and setbacks as opportunities for learning and growth, keeping your "why" or North Star as your guiding force.

7. **Seek Feedback and Invest in Professional Development**: Pursue constructive feedback to identify areas for improvement and demonstrate a commitment to growth and development. Volunteer for projects aligned with your skills and interests and invest in professional development through industry trends, workshops, and certifications.

The Deep Dive

3 Personal **SMART** goals to Navigate the Deep Waters (Specific, Measurable, Achievable, Relevant, and Time-Bound)

READER TAKEAWAY 1

_____
_____
_____
_____
_____
_____

READER TAKEAWAY 2

_____
_____
_____
_____
_____
_____

READER TAKEAWAY 3

_____
_____
_____
_____
_____
_____

NOTES

THREE

LEAD THROUGH AMBIGUITY

The leaves crunched beneath my sneakers, a familiar soundtrack to a season of change. It was the first week of fall in Maplewood, New Jersey—a time when the world seemed to exhale after the intensity of summer. The trees along Parker Avenue lit up in bursts of copper and crimson, each leaf dancing toward the ground like a quiet celebration of transition.

That was high school. A place where change was both seasonal and deeply personal. Where hallway conversations jumped from academics, music, and sports, and cafeteria tables became melting pots of skin tones, accents, and unspoken stories. Columbia High School wasn't just my academic training ground—it was where I unknowingly began my education in ambiguity.

In that environment, you learned how to read a room. Not the kind you'd find in a quarterly town hall meeting, but the kind where understanding someone's silence mattered more than winning the argument. You learned to switch languages—figuratively and literally—to connect across cultures. You got comfortable being uncomfortable. Because no one looked like everyone, and yet we all belonged. That early exposure to diversity didn't just shape my social instincts; it sharpened the tool every leader needs when certainty disappears: empathy.

Fast-forward two decades. I'm seated in a 37th-floor conference room in lower Manhattan. Floor-to-ceiling windows offer a god-like view of the skyline, but the fog inside the room is what I'm focused on. A product launch has missed its deadline. New regulations are dropping with no precedent. Our best developer just gave notice. And now, all eyes are on me—not for answers, but for clarity.

This is the new reality for mid-level professionals: being in the middle of the chaos. You're not the junior staff asking what's next. You're not the CEO setting the north star. You are the bridge. The translator. The calm voice when the data is incomplete and the stakes are high. No longer just executing someone else's vision—you're shaping your own, often without a playbook.

And yet, I've come to realize that ambiguity isn't something to fear. It's something to master. Especially in a world where your teams span time zones, your customers speak in code, and your success depends less on having the right answers and more on asking the right questions.

Back when I was in school, no one taught us how to manage a reorg, lead hybrid teams, navigate corporate politics, or translate vision into velocity. Technology, personal finance, career strategy—these were electives in the real world, not on the curriculum. As a result, I decided to give back. I wrote *Wisdom on the Way to Wall Street: 22 Steps to Navigate Your Road to Success* and shared it in classrooms. I realized the audience wasn't just students. It was professionals like you—leaders navigating complexity, recalibrating in real time, trying to grow when the path isn't linear.

Understanding the stages of your career and identifying its transitions is necessary. When becoming a first-time manager, this move is often a big challenge in your career. This shift requires moving from self-mastery to empowering others and relinquishing control to achieve collective results. For new managers, investing in team development through skill-building opportunities, mentorship, and professional growth is paramount. Effective communication—embracing open dialogue, offering constructive feedback, and active listening are essential for fostering a cohesive team environment.

Conflict is unavoidable in any workplace. Learning to address and resolve it well is fundamental. Encouraging open communication is important. Mediating when needed and guiding the team to agreement are crucial skills. Leadership is not just about navigating calm waters. True leadership thrives in ambiguity, recognizing change as constant and valuing diverse perspectives for optimal outcomes. Leaders prioritize listening over speaking, making tough decisions based on customer needs, data insights, and team respect, rather than seeking popularity.

Consider the legendary explorers of the past who faced uncertainty, risks, challenges, and the unknown, yet made groundbreaking discoveries. Now, reflect on the tools at your disposal for making the greatest impact in business. Uncertainty is constant, requiring leaders to anchor themselves in key principles and be unwavering voices for their teams and communities.

Leaders must adapt and adjust their sails, much like sailors navigating their boats using the wind to stay on course. If you veer off course, quick action is key to finding your way. Even if it means a needed turn, that may become a crisis. Embracing a "fail forward" mindset, acknowledging mistakes, and taking responsibility for decisions are vital. Problems do not age well. Leaders need foresight to fix them before they get worse.

While some challenges can be anticipated, not all can be foreseen. Treat errors as valuable data points, learn from them, and move forward. Concentrate on what you can control, and let go of what lies beyond your influence. You wouldn't load unnecessary cargo onto your ship. Maintain lean operations to ease swift adaptation to unforeseen circumstances.

Navigating ambiguity demands adaptability and flexibility in leadership, emphasizing regular, early communication with stakeholders to keep them informed. Strategic leaders rely on intuition and thorough research during uncertain times, maintaining a positive mindset and authenticity in their approach. Authentic leadership influences organizational culture and inspires teams to excel in new endeavors. Leading through ambiguity in a corporate setting means effectively guiding teams and making decisions despite uncertainty, incomplete information, or rapidly changing circumstances. It requires adaptability, resilience, and strategic thinking to navigate complexity and drive progress.

As a front-runner, you must take responsibility for the success of those under your leadership team. If a new team member is facing challenges in their role, it reflects on your leadership. You have the duty to ensure that they have all the necessary tools for success. If a subordinate is up for a promotion but falls short, you must check to see if they have the right projects to show they're ready for the next level. Have you communicated their achievements to the senior management team? Have you championed their work? Have you provided them with the platform to operate at an elevated level? These considerations should shape your leadership approach. The ship's captain is the top authority, but they rely on a crew to reach the goal. However, arrogance, lack of likeability, and narrow vision can derail any leader, potentially ending their career prematurely.

Managing change within a company, especially when introducing new tools, requires meticulous planning. Start with smaller teams to explain your vision and gain their commitment. Only after that, expand the changes to larger parts of the organization. Focus on enhancing user experience with empathy, understanding stakeholder challenges, and offering inclusive solutions. Articulate your vision and cultivate alliances with stakeholders who share your perspective. Those who need more time to embrace change might not be the leaders of change. They need time to adapt.

Once you have the team's support, you can introduce the change gradually. You do this across the organization, team by team. Change often reveals chances to improve efficiency and skills. In some cases, it also allows for streamlining with automation.

While driving change, it's common to experience moments of impostor syndrome, despite your accomplishments. This psychological phenomenon involves questioning one's abilities and feeling undeserving of success despite evidence of competence. Many professionals, across various fields, face this challenge. During moments of self-doubt, reflect on the hard work and sacrifices of those who came before you. If you've earned a job interview or offer, it's because of your qualifications and merits—have confidence in your abilities without relying on external validation.

Belief in your abilities should be balanced with diligence and modesty, key elements for a successful career. Let the quality of your work speak for itself. Don't consider any task beneath you. Doing smaller tasks builds a strong reputation. It also adds to your credibility. This makes you more reliable for bigger duties. Adopt the practice of promising and surpassing expectations in execution. Upon completing a task, seek extra responsibilities, and foster career advancement. While humility is imperative, acknowledge your achievements modestly and allow others to recognize your contributions. Embrace humility as a tool for growth as you navigate your career and address any blind spots that arise.

7 LIFE RAFTS TO NAVIGATE CAREER CURRENTS WHILE LEADING THROUGH AMBIGUITY

1. **Self-Mastery to Building Teams by Empowering Others**: Understanding career stages and transitions is crucial. Moving from self-mastery to empowering others challenges new managers to focus on team development. This shift offers opportunities for skill-building, mentorship, and professional growth.

2. **Resolving Conflict Requires Leading in Ambiguity**: Effective leaders excel in navigating ambiguity and addressing conflicts. They encourage open communication, mediate when necessary, and make tough, sometimes unpopular, decisions based on data and respect for their team. They see change as constant and value diverse perspectives.

3. **Adaptability and Resilience Through Leadership**: Leaders must be adaptable and flexible, maintaining lean operations and focusing on what they can control. Embracing a "fail forward" mindset, learning from mistakes, and continuously improving are crucial in uncertain times.

4. **Leading as Your Authentic Self**: Authenticity is fundamental to effective leadership. Leading as your authentic self positively impacts organizational culture, fostering team performance and individual growth aligned with authentic values.

5. **Managing Effective Change**: Managing change requires careful planning, starting with smaller teams, and expanding gradually with empathy and understanding. Effective change management involves explaining the vision, securing commitment, and using data and testing to inform decisions.

6. **Overcoming Impostor Syndrome**: Leaders should be aware of impostor syndrome, which causes self-doubt despite evident competence. Balancing confidence in one's abilities with humility and diligence are instrumental for sustained career success. Reflecting on the sacrifices and achievements of ancestors can help combat feelings of inadequacy.

7. **Utilizing Humility and Professionalism**: Humility is key to professionalism. Embrace humility by undertaking diverse tasks, allowing your work quality to shine. This builds credibility and reliability, paving the way for larger responsibilities and leadership roles.

3 Personal **SMART** goals to Navigate the Deep Waters (Specific, Measurable, Achievable, Relevant, and Time-Bound)

READER TAKEAWAY 1

_____
_____
_____
_____
_____
_____

READER TAKEAWAY 2

_____
_____
_____
_____
_____
_____

READER TAKEAWAY 3

_____
_____
_____
_____
_____
_____

NOTES

FOUR

CHECK YOUR BLIND SPOTS

It's late October in the Northeast. You're behind the wheel, driving alone just before sunset. The sun dips low, casting a golden hue across the highway. The trees lining the road are ablaze in color—crimson, burnt orange, golden yellow—gently letting go of their leaves like nature exhaling. The rhythmic hum of tires on pavement creates a calm, meditative focus. You feel in control. You're in your lane, making good time.

Then—a flash of movement in your side mirror. A car, tucked just out of view, suddenly veers into your lane. You jolt, swerve, slam the brakes. Heart pounding. You never saw it coming. That hidden car is your blind spot causing a collision ahead. Tires screech, and chaos ensues momentarily. Bystanders rush to help, police arrive to file reports, and an ambulance speeds away with an injured passenger. Miraculously, everyone survives, but the cars are mangled beyond recognition.

In your career, the same can happen. Midway through your professional journey, you may be cruising—building on years of experience, trusted by peers, valued by your organization. But blind spots—unspoken assumptions, complacency, ignored signals—can still cause major disruption. Maybe it's a missed promotion. A reorg you didn't anticipate. A feedback loop you never opened.

This chapter is a wake-up call. Just like a seasoned driver learns to glance over their shoulder, you too must build the habit of checking your professional blind spots. Because awareness isn't just a skill—it's your safeguard on the road to growth.

Reflecting on your journey is invaluable in business. Confronting your blind spots humbly is a critical step toward success. Every journey involves solving problems, from weather obstacles to maintenance issues. The ability to continuously adapt, renew, and refresh is essential amidst life's challenges and obstacles. Embrace the role of a proactive problem solver.

As you navigate the ship, vigilance and knowledge are your allies. The more you know about your organization and how it functions, the more effective you become. This knowledge empowers you to streamline operations, eliminate duplicative tasks, and introduce automation for efficiency. This frees up your team's time for strategic initiatives.

As the team works cohesively, pay attention to caution signs and detours. Please don't ignore them. Embrace the uniqueness and varying speeds of each individual's journey. Avoid simply mimicking others. When you lead and build great teams, effectively communicate your organization's vision and how your team's work aligns with it.

It's vital to understand what inspires each of your team members. What do they seek to gain from their work? By helping them see value in their contributions, you'll motivate them to be more committed and productive. This fosters a sense of belonging and purpose within the team, encouraging them to identify and address blind spots to prevent future crises proactively.

Empowerment is another fundamental element in building successful teams to help check organizational blind spots. The objective is to foster a culture where your team can make decisions independently, ensuring business continuity even in your absence. Adapting to constant market and product changes is crucial. Regular meetings with your manager and their manager keep you informed about organizational developments, enabling you to provide your team with pertinent updates and a sense of collective purpose.

Prioritize regular coaching sessions and individual meetings with team members to discuss priorities; a weekly or monthly cadence, depending on how mature the team is, helps promote cohesion and synergy across projects.

Encourage a collaborative culture that embraces innovative ideas and ensures psychological safety for all team members to freely express their thoughts. Success in business hinges largely on assembling the right team whose synergy drives efficiency and economic success.

While performing at a high level and checking your blind spots, be sure to pay attention to your team's well-being. Encourage self-care and mental health awareness, and ensure each team member feels fulfilled in their role. Support those whose skills have outgrown their current position by facilitating internal mobility within the organization to retain top talent and avoid costly turnover.

In today's dynamic business landscape, technological shifts can create blind spots, necessitating continuous upskilling to remain relevant and effective. Stay informed about industry trends through professional development activities such as reading, attending conferences, and networking with experts. Anticipate future challenges and customer needs to innovate and provide forward-thinking solutions, even if met with initial resistance. Embrace your vision and ideas confidently—they define your unique brand and could lead to groundbreaking opportunities with persistence and perseverance.

Checking your blind spots doesn't just prevent conflicts; it helps keep them at bay. Yet, when conflicts do arise, regular reflection and self-assessment are important for identifying and mitigating personal biases. You must actively challenge your assumptions and those of your team. Do this by asking probing questions to encourage critical thinking. Consider alternative perspectives and potential unintended consequences before making decisions. This will ensure a growth mindset culture with an emphasis on continuous improvement.

Externally, when working with clients, prioritize understanding their needs. Skills like self-awareness, self-regulation, and strong social skills are invaluable in navigating conflicts effectively. Regularly reflect on your decisions, actions, and leadership style, seeking ways to improve and considering how others perceive your behavior.

Encouraging open and candid feedback is another effective method to identify blind spots. Solicit feedback from various sources, including your team, peers, and superiors. Embrace diverse perspectives on your leadership style, communication, and decision-making processes to uncover any potential blind spots. Participating in 360-degree assessments offers comprehensive feedback from different angles, further illuminating areas for improvement. Be sure to pay close attention to the constructive feedback received.

Executives can leverage these tactics to find and fix blind spots. This will improve their decision-making and drive success.

The Deep Dive

Navigating your career's blind spots can be challenging but crucial to your growth and success. Remember, a smooth journey involves checking your blind spots often. You must stay vigilant, and adapt to the changes and challenges ahead. Your career journey is about growth. These principles will serve you well as you navigate the twists and turns of success.

7 LIFE RAFTS TO NAVIGATE CAREER CURRENTS BY CHECKING YOUR BLIND SPOTS

1. **Check your Blind Spots**: Just as drivers must check their blind spots to avoid accidents, professionals should continuously identify and address their blind spots to prevent career setbacks.

2. **Watch for Caution Signs and Detours**: Pay attention to warning signs and be willing to adjust your course when necessary to navigate challenges effectively.

3. **Embrace Reflection and Adaptation**: Regular self-reflection and adapting to career changes are crucial for personal and professional growth. Understanding and confronting your limitations lead to success.

4. **Motivate Your Team to Help Check Blind Spots**: Foster a culture where your team can make decisions independently. Help them see the value in their work to create autonomy and commitment, boosting productivity and morale.

5. **Encourage Open Feedback and Diverse Perspectives**: Gather feedback from various sources, including team members, peers, and superiors, to uncover potential blind spots. Embrace diverse perspectives to enhance your decision-making process.

6. **Focus on Well-being and Career Growth**: Pay attention to your team's well-being and career aspirations. Support their growth within the organization to retain top talent

and avoid the costs associated with hiring and retraining new staff.

7. **Foster a Collaborative and Innovative Culture**: Encourage a culture of collaboration, innovation, and psychological safety. Regular coaching and meetings, combined with a focus on individual priorities, promote synergies, and drive success in projects and initiatives.

3 Personal **SMART** goals to Navigate the Deep Waters (Specific, Measurable, Achievable, Relevant, and Time-Bound)

READER TAKEAWAY 1

_____
_____
_____
_____
_____

READER TAKEAWAY 2

_____
_____
_____
_____
_____

READER TAKEAWAY 3

_____
_____
_____
_____
_____

NOTES

FIVE

DON'T PROCRASTINATE TO PIVOT

Flashback to those adrenaline-fueled Friday afternoons—school bags tossed aside, helmets strapped on, the hum of go-karts revving to life. You and your friends lined up on the track, ready to conquer the circuit. For twenty-five thrilling minutes, you zigzagged through tight turns, wind in your face, heart pounding with each lap.

The most exciting stretch is a fork in the road.

Left lane meant safety—familiar curves, predictable pace. But if you veered right, you hit the turbo zone: a smooth curve that let you pick up an extra fifteen miles per hour. It shaved minutes off your race and left everyone else in your rearview mirror.

This moment at the fork mirrors your professional crossroads. Mid-career often brings decisions laced with doubt—stay safe in what you know, or take a chance on reinvention? That burst of speed? It's not luck. It's the reward for pivoting early and decisively. Whether it's upskilling, changing industries, or launching something new, delays only stall your momentum. In this race, hesitation has a cost—but timely pivots can be the slingshot that propels you to the front of the pack.

When do you pivot?

Knowing when to pivot—whether in your role, company, or team—is crucial. It's easy to grow comfortable or complacent, but real growth often lies outside our comfort zone. Discomfort can signal that it's time to pivot.

Consider these key questions when evaluating a potential career pivot:

1. Have you been at your current organization or in your current role for an extended period (3-5 years)?
2. Do you have strong relationships at work? Do you have sponsorship and advocates there?
3. Are you set up for success in your current role?
4. Do you wake up feeling energized to go to work?
5. Do you experience the dreaded "Sunday Scaries"?

6. Do you feel adequately challenged in your current role?
7. Are there opportunities for growth in your present position?
8. When you look at your manager, do you see yourself in their role?

These questions offer insights into your career trajectory. Specializing too narrowly in a fast-changing job market can lead to being pigeonholed. The importance of reskilling and evolving cannot be overstated. Continuous learning is a cornerstone of a successful career.

This might involve reading new books, acquiring certifications, or returning to school. Curiosity and problem-solving skills are invaluable in adapting and staying relevant in your career. For example, recognizing the shift in finance towards technology, I chose to pursue an Executive MBA after fifteen years in my career, enhancing my skills, and staying ahead of industry changes.

When considering a career pivot, thorough market research is essential. Identify growth opportunities that align with your skills. Develop a detailed plan outlining short-term and long-term goals, along with timelines and strategies to overcome expected challenges.

Revise your resume and professional materials to highlight relevant skills and achievements that support your new career direction. Drawing from my background in capital market sales, corporate finance, enterprise risk management, innovation, consulting, and product management, I successfully transitioned into financial technology. This shift showed professional growth and responded to broader social trends. Society now prizes efficiency through technology like online grocery shopping and ride-hailing apps. I saw the potential of financial technology as a driving force in the years ahead so made sure to embrace this pivotal career move.

To pivot careers successfully, employ strategic approaches such as setting clear, measurable objectives, and defining milestones with implementation deadlines. Break down the transition into manageable tasks and allocate adequate resources to support execution. Address potential challenges and risks while highlighting opportunities for growth and innovation. Empower team members with the authority, autonomy, and resources necessary for effective execution, as you pivot. Continuously monitor progress using Key Performance Indicators (KPIs) and remain adaptable, adjusting strategies based on real-time feedback.

Always maintain a positive mindset that new opportunities are around the corner. In your career journey's vast ocean, currents and waves may steer you into unpredictable waters. Understand that while rejection is part of the process, it's crucial to align any opportunity with your values and long-term vision. Research potential employers thoroughly, considering their culture and the people you'll work with. Aim to leave your current role on a positive note, nurturing relationships with former colleagues and managers.

Diligently researching your prospective colleagues, both internally and externally, is a smart pivot strategy. When making a smart pivot, consider the North Star of your career. Where and who do you want to be before retirement? While it's a long-term question, it can guide in making strategic moves.

Document your career plan, outlining your current position, desired destination, and steps to achieve your goals. While plans may evolve, having a clear roadmap and staying committed to your vision is pivotal. Focus on the process and execution, celebrating milestones along the way.

If you can't secure opportunities internally that allow you to use your talents, it may be time to pivot. Remember, it's not all or nothing. Flexibility is fundamental to building collaborative partnerships. You must remain committed to decisions that align with the organization's vision. Remember, you're part of a larger mission, potentially influencing cost reduction, increased revenue, innovative client solutions, or operational efficiency within the company.

Keeping your resume updated is essential, whether you are actively job searching or thriving in your current role. Continuously assess your career journey, the job market, and your long-term vision. Stay open to new opportunities and excel in interviews. Confidently negotiate your job offer once you're certain about your career pivot.

When it comes to interviews, always be your authentic self. Prepare well. Research the company and know your resume. Stay informed about industry trends and prepare thoughtful questions for the interviewers. Remember, they're humans too, so approach the interviews as a conversation to assess mutual fit.

Once you shine, throughout the interviews and when you receive an offer, always negotiate. Consider compensation, remote work options, benefits, and vacation days. Research market compensation for your level and skills to negotiate confidently without undervaluing yourself. Active listening and knowing when to compromise are great negotiation tactics.

After your new opportunity is in hand concentrate on setting a strong foundation in your first ninety days. Focus on learning about key stakeholders, your organization's culture, values, and expectations. From three to six months, start making a significant impact by addressing barriers, building your network, and enhancing processes. In the six- to twelve-month timeframe, concentrate on talent development and discuss your personal growth trajectory within the organization.

Pivoting your career is a bold move. Yet, it can be motivating. Keep your skills sharp and your mind open to new opportunities. In business, value creation often leads to financial rewards, so be prepared for challenges that may arise unexpectedly. Embrace a survivor's mindset, staying adaptable even during smooth sailing as winds and storms are inevitable.

Matthew C. Meade

Embrace adaptation! Just as changing course in a go-kart race can lead to exhilarating speed, a strategic career pivot can propel you toward success and purpose. By making the right pivots at the right time, you're steering your path to success, growth, and great purpose. Famous explorers changed their paths for many reasons. This led to both success and challenges.

Remember the words of Martin Luther King Jr., "Keep Your Eyes on The Prize!" and when working hard remember to take care of yourself as you chart a purposeful new course in your career.

7 LIFE RAFTS TO NAVIGATE CAREER CURRENTS WHILE NOT PROCRASTINATING THE PIVOT

1. **Recognize the Pivotal Moments**: Just like in a go-kart race, there are moments in your career where you have to make choices that could significantly impact your trajectory. Recognizing these pivotal moments is crucial.

2. **Make Sure to Assess Your Current Situation**: Ask yourself important questions about your current role, relationships at work, and whether you feel challenged and energized. This self-assessment can help you determine if it's time to make a career pivot.

3. **Research and Plan for Your Pivot**: Before making a career pivot, thoroughly research the market. Identify growth opportunities that align with your skills and create a detailed plan outlining your goals, timeline, and expected challenges.

4. **Set Clear Goals and Deadlines**: Define specific, measurable objectives and break down the pivot into manageable tasks. Allocate resources effectively, address potential challenges, and empower team members during the transition.

5. **Utilize Effective Strategies to Pivot**: Set SMART goals, allocate resources, communicate with stakeholders, utilize your network, and foster collaboration to ensure a successful career pivot.

6. **Maintain a Positive Mindset**: Understand that rejection is a part of the process, but stay positive and keep moving forward. You can focus on finding opportunities that align with your values and long-term vision.

7. **Stay True to Your Vision**: Write down your career plan and stay committed to it. Focus on the process and celebrate each milestone as you progress towards your goals.

3 Personal **SMART** goals to Navigate the Deep Waters (Specific, Measurable, Achievable, Relevant, and Time-Bound)

READER TAKEAWAY 1

READER TAKEAWAY 2

READER TAKEAWAY 3

Matthew C. Meade

NOTES

SIX

YOUR BEST SELF REQUIRES SELF-CARE

Early in my career on Wall Street, it was one of those marathon days—the kind that starts before sunrise and refuses to end. I was knee-deep in a critical client report, fueled only by ambition and the growing weight of expectation. The clock ticked past 10 pm, and I hadn't eaten a real meal or stepped outside once. I'd been staring at my screen since 7 am, determined to push through. But something shifted.

My brain—usually sharp and nimble—felt sluggish. Simple tasks took longer. Mistakes started sneaking in. And then it hit me: I wasn't operating at my best—I was just... operating.

That night, I chose to step away. I shut my laptop, left the office haze behind, and returned home. I dimmed the lights, queued up a jazz playlist, and lit a single candle. The silence was restorative. For the first time in days, I exhaled. I allowed myself a full reset—mentally, physically, and emotionally.

The next afternoon, I returned to my desk with fresh eyes and sharper focus. What had felt like an uphill battle now flowed with ease. The difference? Rest.

Mid-career professionals often equate productivity with perseverance. Often, thinking that staying late and skipping breaks is a badge of honor. The truth is, your performance is only as strong as your personal foundation. Self-care isn't indulgence—it's infrastructure. It's the unseen scaffolding of peak performance.

Wellness, movement, meaningful nutrition, and sleep—these aren't side quests. They are your main storyline.

In the blur of meetings, deadlines, and life's never-ending notifications, it's easy to forget that you are the engine powering it all. To lead effectively, think clearly, and sustain impact, you must be present. Presence requires balance, a crucial yet often undervalued art. That means stepping out of autopilot, tuning in to what your body and mind need, and making space for the quiet moments that bring you back to center.

Don't live only for the weekend or wait for burnout to slow you down. Instead, start reclaiming the present moment. It's the most powerful—and often most neglected—form of leadership you can practice.

Exercise is a fundamental element of a fulfilling life. Incorporate exercise into your routine, monitoring progress with fitness trackers and smartwatches for optimal health benefits. Aim for at least three 45-minute sessions per week to enhance sleep quality, reduce anxiety, maintain weight, improve strength, and boost memory. Even short bursts of activity, like a brisk daily walk, can significantly enhance productivity and overall health by reducing the risk of chronic illnesses like heart disease and diabetes.

Hydration is equally important. Research recommends men should drink about 3.7 liters (125 ounces) and women should drink 2.7 liters (91 ounces) of water daily. Stay hydrated to maintain peak mental and physical performance throughout the day.

Dedicate yourself to hard work, but maintain clear boundaries between your professional and personal life. Despite life's busyness blurring these lines, safeguarding your well-being is essential for sustained effectiveness. Establish personal KPIs outside of work, encompassing moments with family and friends, annual traditions, vacations, sleep, and workouts. Avoid letting work consume you to the point where you lose sight of yourself and what truly matters.

For me, this involves staying true to my faith and prioritizing the well-being of my family. Your North Star—your guiding light—is too precious to compromise. Never forget who you are or compromise your values. Achieving your best self in both personal and professional realms requires finding balance: living to work and working to live.

Don't hesitate to take days off when you need a break. Furthermore, be intentional about getting seven to eight hours of sleep per night. Research shows that those who sleep adequately are about thirty percent better at decision-making than those who sleep less. A well-rested mind enhances your effectiveness, benefiting both colleagues and your organization.

The best version of you is one that embodies self-care. It's your responsibility, your job, to be kind to yourself. Remember, mistakes are part of the journey, and forgiveness—both for others and yourself—is necessary. Careers rarely follow a straight path. As you navigate your career, embrace the lessons that come your way. They are valuable. Make self-care a priority, recognizing that you can't give from an empty well. When overwhelmed, unplug, reset, and protect your energy. Invest daily in activities that rejuvenate your physical and mental well-being, enabling you to contribute effectively to larger goals.

In your career journey, you'll find that the ultimate goal is to build something greater. A lasting impact is one of the essential pillars of your fulfillment. Engage in philanthropy and work to improve society. Look for non-profits that share your passion and values. Take the lead in helping them fulfill their mission. Lead with empathy, purpose, and passion. Ask yourself, "What does the world need to become a better place?" If you see something that has not yet been realized, you can make it happen. Brave leaders do not shy away from challenges.

Think of wealth as a composition of great health, impact, and relationships. Pursue and influence rather than solely financial gain. Innovate and challenge the status quo, contributing positively to society as a producer, not just a consumer. Your legacy is defined by how many lives you've enriched. Treat everyone with respect and support, helping them achieve their full potential from wherever they are on their journey.

Remember, you are the product of your ancestors' dreams. Honor this legacy by striving for self-actualization and a higher purpose. You transition from life once in physical form, so live daily; prioritize self-care and focus on living fully. If you had only an hour left, you'd cherish moments with loved ones—not work tasks or products. Make this realization a daily priority.

Throughout a career, prioritize self-care to preserve well-being, manage stress, and maintain peak performance. Effective time management is key; schedule regular breaks and set clear boundaries around work hours to prevent burnout. Delegate tasks when necessary, and avoid overcommitting.

Inhale, exhale.

Practice mindfulness and stress-reduction techniques. Dedicate time to meditation, deep breathing, or muscle relaxation each day. Nurture relationships outside of work, fostering connections with friends, family, and colleagues. Surround yourself with supportive individuals who understand the demands of your role. Invest in personal and professional development through workshops and seminars. Prioritize workouts to improve health and mood. By embracing self-care, leaders like you can keep a healthy work-life balance and well-being throughout your career.

 **7 LIFE RAFTS TO NAVIGATE CAREER CURRENTS WHILE REQUIRING SELF-CARE**

1. **Importance of Self-Care:** Self-care is foundational for a successful professional journey. Neglecting it can lead to burnout, reduced productivity, and poor decision-making. It's essential to balance work demands with personal well-being.

2. **Create Positive Habits:** Building positive habits related to wellness, exercise, nutrition, and sleep will form the foundation for long-term well-being. These habits contribute to improved mental and physical health, essential for professional performance.

3. **Benefits of Physical Activity:** Regular exercise is crucial for mental and physical health. It enhances sleep, reduces anxiety, controls weight, and improves memory. Aim for at least three 45-minute exercise sessions per week.

4. **Benefits of Hydration:** Proper hydration is vital for overall health and productivity. Men should aim for 3.7 liters (13 cups) and women for 2.7 liters (9 cups) of water daily.

5. **Benefits of Adequate Sleep:** Prioritizing 7-8 hours of sleep per night improves decision-making and productivity. Research shows that those who sleep adequately are about thirty percent better at decision-making than those who sleep less.

6. **Establish Personal KPIs for Optimal Balance:** Setting boundaries between work and personal life is fundamental

for long-term well-being and effectiveness. Establish personal KPIs that include family time, traditions, vacations, and self-care activities.

7. **Practice Mindfulness, Presence, and Purpose:** Being present in the moment is important for reducing stress and improving performance. As you build something, practice a greater focus on leading with empathy, purpose, and passion.

3 Personal **SMART** goals to Navigate the Deep Waters (Specific, Measurable, Achievable, Relevant, and Time-Bound)

READER TAKEAWAY 1

_____
_____
_____
_____
_____
_____

READER TAKEAWAY 2

_____
_____
_____
_____
_____
_____

READER TAKEAWAY 3

_____
_____
_____
_____
_____
_____

NOTES

SEVEN

THE REST ASHORE

In the northeastern United States, winter doesn't ask permission—it arrives with force and clarity. The snow doesn't whisper; it declares. It piles up silently overnight, transforming familiar streets into blank canvases of white. Trees bend under the weight. Cars disappear under soft, silent drifts. And yet, in those still, frozen mornings, something incredible happens: people come out.

Neighbors emerge from their homes bundled in layers—shovels in hand, breath visible in the icy air. There's no memo. No Slack notification. Just instinct. Just care. You see a father clearing a path for the elderly couple next door. A teenager helps dig out a stranger's buried sedan. Someone starts a slow clap when the street's last patch of sidewalk is finally cleared.

Then, just as suddenly, the modern workday begins. You peel off your gloves and step into a different kind of storm—this one filled with inboxes, deadlines, and decision trees. Your manager pings you with a "quick question." A client wants numbers that weren't due for another week. A direct report needs guidance. You move seamlessly from snow boots to spreadsheets, trading your shovel for your laptop.

And when the snow doesn't let up—when it becomes clear a second round of digging will be needed—you return to it, shovel in hand, muscles sore, heart full. Because the last thing anyone wants is to let the snow sit, turn to ice, and become a hidden threat in the morning. It's not about heroism. It's about responsibility. It's about showing up.

The irony is that these days, while exhausting, are the ones you remember. They strip away the noise. They remind you who you are beneath the deadlines. You led, you served, and you endured. Not for recognition, but because something deeper called you to act.

And then—finally—the day is done.

You hang your coat. You close your laptop. You exhale.

You change into flannel pajamas and slide between freshly washed sheets. The heat hums softly in the background. A mug

The Deep Dive

of hot chocolate warms your hands as the snow continues to fall outside, quietly, like applause you don't need to hear. You're not worried about tomorrow—not tonight. Because you've done the work. You've shown up for your team, your community, yourself.

This is what self-actualization feels like in the corporate world—not a grand TED Talk moment or a trophy on the shelf, but a quiet, settled knowing: *I'm aligned. I've given what I had. I can rest now.*

Because true fulfillment isn't found in doing everything.

It's found in doing the right things—with purpose—and then, letting yourself be at peace.

And so, you sleep.

Assured.

Morning comes, another day. Keep pressing on, for the journey is far from over. The path ahead might seem uncertain. You are searching for new opportunities, transitioning to new roles, and pivoting your career. During these times, lean on your network. You'll find people who are eager to help and curious about your journey. You've built a board of directors through your connections with thought leaders across various industries. They can be valuable resources. Reach out to them, inquire about their well-being, and share your career aspirations.

I recall meeting with over two hundred leaders in six months. We discussed our visions for the financial technology sector to see if our goals were aligned. We aimed to build groundbreaking solutions that could reshape the industry. Some shared the same vision, while others were miles away from it. Conversations ranged from background updates to sharing visionary insights to discussing global team-building, new market solutions, and influencing large-scale organizations. Each dialogue required curiosity, honesty, and integrity, leaving me energized when they resonated.

In your journey, find motivation and inspiration in these conversations. Every interaction holds potential, opening doors and forging collaborations that leave a lasting impact on your industry.

As you think of growth transitions, begin by outlining your career goals. Include specifics like desired company culture, preferred colleagues, and projects you're passionate about. Balance ambition with feasibility—include moonshots, but ensure your goals are attainable. Strike a balance between optimism, resilience, and realism as you navigate your path forward.

If you're seeking to build something new, consider the problems you or your potential customers face. Always look for unmet needs in your industry but gather data to solidify the need. You can address them with transformative solutions. You might also explore business ideas or innovations that succeeded in one country. They could potentially find success in another country.

Throughout this process, trust in yourself and be prepared to take calculated risks. Speed may lead to success in some instances, while in others, patience and strategy are pivotal. Embrace the ups and downs, navigating career currents with perseverance and flexibility. Be open to unexpected opportunities, trusting in the natural order of your life's journey toward new horizons.

You have surely worked very hard to advance in your career. Now, it's vital to keep up your progress. Sustainable leadership requires resilience and adaptability. It also needs effective strategies for beating obstacles and maintaining long-term success. Build a strong support system. Surround yourself with mentors, peers, and trusted advisors. They offer guidance and perspective. Foster relationships both within and outside your organization to access mentorship and encouragement. Cultivate a collaborative work environment where colleagues share insights and support each other towards common goals.

Focus on work-life balance by setting boundaries, taking breaks, and delegating tasks to prevent burnout. Make time for hobbies and interests outside of work to nurture personal fulfillment. Commit to lifelong learning and embrace challenges as opportunities for growth. Stay agile while maintaining a clear strategy, and informed about industry trends to remain competitive.

Reflect on the big picture—every day is a gift and a chance to build something new. Embrace change and new beginnings as catalysts for personal and professional growth. Find something you excel at, love to do, and that people value you for. Work as if you were the owner of your path, and as you rise, remain grounded.

As you elevate, always remember, at times when you're high - remain humble. At times when you feel low – remain hopeful. Never forget those who paved the way for you. Always be willing to pay it forward for the next generation as you reach success and sail off into the sunset.

 **7 LIFE RAFTS TO NAVIGATE CAREER CURRENTS AS THE REST IS ASHORE**

1. **Power in Community Resilience:** In harsh winters, communities come together to support each other. This highlights the importance of unity and assistance during challenging times.

2. **Balance Your Goal Setting:** Encouragement is given to set both achievable goals and ambitious "moonshots," while maintaining a balance to avoid overwhelming oneself with unattainable objectives.

3. **Take Risks and Foster Self-Belief:** Embrace risks and have faith in your abilities. Recognize when to accelerate and when to slow down, trusting in how the journey's unfolding.

4. **Identify Transformative Opportunities:** Seek unmet needs in your industry and explore innovative solutions to address them, potentially drawing inspiration from successful ventures in other regions.

5. **Always Network:** There's significance in leveraging your network during times of transition, seeking advice and opportunities from a diverse range of connections, including thought leaders and industry professionals.

6. **Live in the Present:** Cherish each day as an opportunity for growth and change. Stay grounded in success, maintain humility, and remain hopeful during challenges. Acknowledge those who have influenced your journey.

7. **Exercise Gratefulness, Humility, and Generosity:** Have immense gratitude for every day, humility in success, and a willingness to give back and pave the way for future generations, even as you achieve personal success.

3 Personal **SMART** goals to Navigate the Deep Waters (Specific, Measurable, Achievable, Relevant, and Time-Bound)

READER TAKEAWAY 1

READER TAKEAWAY 2

READER TAKEAWAY 3

NOTES

www.ingramcontent.com/pod-product-compliance
Lightning Source LLC
Chambersburg PA
CBHW060621080526
44585CB00013B/938